# Joy's Choice

by Joaquin Garcia
illustrated by Liz Wolf

Practice Decodable 79

McGraw Hill Education

Bothell, WA • Chicago, IL • Columbus, OH • New York, NY

**MHEonline.com**



Send all inquiries to:
McGraw-Hill Education
8787 Orion Place
Columbus, OH 43240

ISBN: 978-0-02-131711-0
MHID: 0-02-131711-9

Printed in China.

8 9 10 11 12 DSS 27 26 25 24 23

"I wish I had a cell," said Joy, "and voice mail."

Mom grinned. "You are too little, Joy."

Joy was a bit disappointed. Mom could tell.

"You do have a toy cell," Mom said.

"I know, Mom, and I enjoy it. But the toy is not real," said Joy. "I can't talk to my pals."

Mom thought a bit.

"We can join two empty cans," she explained. "We can use string."

Mom joined two cans. Then she called Joy. Mom's voice was in the can!

"Oh, boy! This is fun!" said Joy. "This is a better choice. It is better than a toy!"